COOL SPY SUPPLIES

Fun Top Secret
Science Projects

Esther Beck

ABDO
Publishing Company

TO ADULT HELPERS

You're invited to assist an up-and-coming scientist! And it will pay off in many ways. Your children can develop new skills, gain confidence, and do some interesting projects while learning about science. What's more, it's going to be a lot of fun!

These projects are designed to let children work independently as much as possible. Encourage them to do whatever they are able to do on their own. Also encourage them to try the variations when supplied and to keep a science journal. Encourage children to think like real scientists.

Before getting started, set some ground rules about using the materials and ingredients. Most important, adult supervision is a must whenever a child uses the stove, chemicals, or dry ice.

So put on your lab coats and stand by. Let your young scientists take the lead. Watch and learn. Praise their efforts. Enjoy the scientific adventure!

VISIT US AT WWW.ABDOPUBLISHING.COM

Published by ABDO Publishing Company, 8000 West 78th Street, Edina, Minnesota 55439. Copyright © 2008 by Abdo Consulting Group, Inc. International copyrights reserved in all countries. No part of this book may be reproduced in any form without written permission from the publisher. The Checkerboard Library™ is a trademark and logo of ABDO Publishing Company.

Printed in the United States.

Design and Production: Mighty Media, Inc.
Art Direction: Kelly Doudna
Photo Credits: Kelly Doudna, iStockphoto/Maartje van Caspel, JupiterImages Corporation, Photodisc, Shutterstock
Series Editor: Pam Price
Consultant: Scott Devens

The following manufacturers/names appearing in this book are trademarks: Conair, Dole, Duracell, Gedney, The Honey House, Kemps, Minute Maid, Panasonic, Scotch, Sharpie, Tropicana

Library of Congress Cataloging-in-Publication Data
Beck, Esther.
  Cool spy supplies : fun top secret science projects / Esther Beck.
    p. cm. -- (Cool science)
  Includes index.
  ISBN 978-1-59928-911-3
  1. Science projects--Juvenile literature. 2. Science--Experiments--Juvenile literature. I. Title.

Q182.3.B4355 2008
507.8--dc22
                              2007005983

Contents

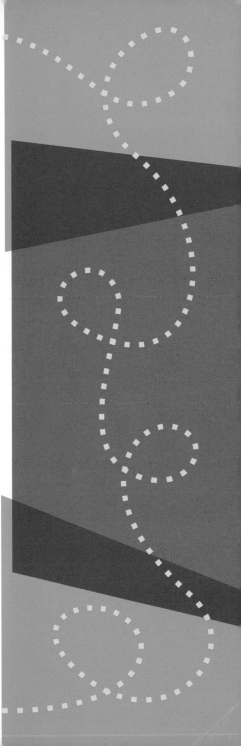

Science Is Cool

Welcome to the cool world of science! Before we get started, let's put on our thinking caps. What do the following things have in common?

- bubbles in soda pop
    - helium balloons that stay up in the air
        - sounds you hear through the headphones of your music player
            - a telescope that makes the faraway moon and stars appear closer
        - choosing your right or left eye to look through a camera viewfinder
    - your ability to balance on one foot

Did you guess that what they have in common is science? That's right, science! When you think of science, maybe you picture someone in a laboratory wearing a long white coat. Perhaps you imagine a scientist hunched over bubbling beakers and test tubes. But science is so much more. Let's take another look.

Soda pop doesn't develop bubbles until you open the container. That's because of a science called chemistry. Chemistry also explains why helium inside a balloon causes it to rise through the air.

You listen to your favorite song through the headphones attached to your music player. You look at the moon and stars through a telescope. Both activities are possible because of a science called physics. Did you know that eyeglasses improve your vision for the same reason telescopes work?

You tend to use the same eye each time you look through a camera viewfinder. You might find it challenging to balance on one foot. The science of biology helps explain why. Did you know it's related to the reason most people use only their left hand or right hand to write?

Broadly defined, science is the study of everything around us. Scientists use experiments and research to figure out how things work and relate to each other. The cool thing about science is that anyone can do it. You don't have to be a scientist in a laboratory to do science. You can do experiments with everyday things!

The Cool Science series introduces you to the world of science. Each book in this series will guide you through several simple experiments and projects with a common theme. The experiments use easy-to-find materials. Step-by-step instructions and photographs help guide your work.

The Scientific Method

Scientists have a special way of working. It is called the scientific method. The scientific method is a series of steps that a scientist follows when trying to learn something. Following the steps makes it more likely that the information you discover will be reliable.

The scientific method is described on the next page. Follow all of the steps. These steps will help you learn the best information possible. And then you can draw an accurate conclusion about what happened. You will even write notes in your own science journal, just like real scientists do!

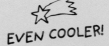

EVEN COOLER!
Check out sections like this one throughout the book. Here you'll find instructions for variations on the project. It might be a suggestion for a different way to do the project. Or it might be a similar project that uses slightly different materials. Either way, it will make your science project even cooler!

1. Observe

Simply pay attention to something. This is called observing. A good way to prepare for the next step is to make up a what, why, or how question about what you observe. For example, let's say you observe that when you open a bottle of soda pop and pour it into a glass, it gets bubbly. Your question could be, How do bubbles get into soda?

2. Hypothesize

Think of a statement that could explain what you have observed. This statement is called a hypothesis. You might remember that you also saw bubbles in your milk when you blew into it with a straw. So your hypothesis might be, I think somebody used a straw to blow into the soda before the bottle was sealed.

3. Test

Test your hypothesis. You do this by conducting an experiment. To test your hypothesis about how bubbles get into soda, you might mix up a recipe, blow into the liquid with a straw, quickly close the container, and then open it back up.

4. Conclude

Draw a conclusion. When you do this, you tie together everything that happened in the previous steps. You report whether the result of the experiment was what you hypothesized. Perhaps there were no bubbles in your soda pop recipe when you reopened the container. You would conclude that blowing through a straw is not how fizz gets into liquids.

Write It Down

A large part of what makes science science is observation. You should observe what happens as you work through an experiment. Scientists observe everything and write notes about it in journals. You can keep a science journal too. All you need is a notebook and a pencil.

At the beginning of each activity in this book, there is a section called "Think Like a Scientist." It contains suggestions about what to record in your science journal. You can predict what you think will happen. You can write down what did happen. And you can draw a conclusion, especially if what really happened is different from what you predicted.

As you do experiments, record things in your journal. You will be working just like a real scientist!

THINK LIKE A SCIENTIST!
Look for a box like this one on the first page of each project. It will give you ideas about what to write in your science journal before, during, and after your experiments. There may be questions about the project. There may be a suggestion about how to look at the project in a different way. Your science journal is the place to keep track of everything!

EVEN COOLER!
You can record more than just words in your journal. You can sketch pictures and make charts. If you have a camera, you can even add photos to your journal!

8

Safe Science

Good scientists practice safe science. Here are some important things to remember.

- Check with an adult before you begin any project. Sometimes you'll need an adult to buy materials or help you handle them for a while. For some projects, an adult will need to help you the whole time. The instructions will say when an adult should assist you.

- Ask for help if you're unsure about how to do something.

- If you or someone else is hurt, tell an adult immediately.

- Read the list of things you'll need. Gather everything before you begin working on a project.

- Don't taste, eat, or drink any of the materials or the results unless the directions say that you can.

- Use protective gear. Scientists wear safety goggles to protect their eyes. They wear gloves to protect their hands from chemicals and possible burns. They wear aprons or lab coats to protect their clothing.

- Clean up when you are finished. That includes putting away materials and washing containers, work surfaces, and your hands.

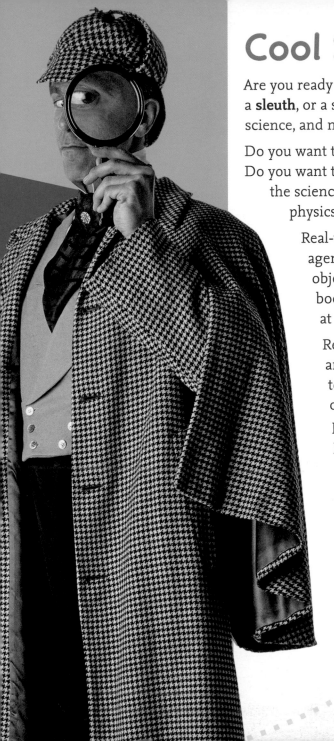

Cool Spy Supplies

Are you ready for some top secret fun? Whether you're a spy, a **sleuth**, or a sneak, science is on your side. That's because science, and mathematics, are **essential** to undercover life.

Do you want to solve a crime? **Forensic science** is for you. Do you want to identify a mystery substance? Chemistry is the science for you! Other areas of science, including physics and biology, also contribute to the field.

Real-world spy science is often cutting-edge. But agents also rely on basic concepts and common objects. You can do the top secret activities in this book with ordinary materials. You can find them at home or at a local store.

Remember to be patient as you work. Redo any activity that doesn't work as you expect it to. Successful spies know that a few minutes of successful spy activity can take hours of preparation. And be sure to track your progress in your science journal. It's a good way to debrief after your top secret science fun.

Materials

You can probably find these supplies around the house.

lemon

small glasses

cotton swabs

paper

lamp with incandescent lightbulb

milk

half-gallon (1.9 l) cartons

scissors or utility knife

pencil

tape

pieces of cardboard

sunglasses

television with a remote control

mirror

marker

magnifying glass

AA batteries

aluminum foil

sturdy paper such as
construction paper

pillow

chair

AT THE CRAFT OR DISCOUNT STORE
You can find these supplies at a craft supply or a discount store.

hot-glue gun

small square mirrors

small round mirrors

pipe cleaners

AT THE ELECTRONICS OR SURPLUS STORE
You can find these supplies at an electronics or a surplus store.

battery holder

alligator wires

DC buzzer

Invisible Inks

TIME: ABOUT 1 HOUR

MATERIALS

lemon half

2 small glasses

cotton swabs

paper

lamp with a 100-watt **incandescent** lightbulb

milk

Secret codes and **ciphers** are common ways for spies to communicate. This activity hides the message entirely. Now that's taking secrecy to an extreme!

CHEMISTRY

THINK LIKE A SCIENTIST!

In your science journal, write your observations about the following questions.

1. Which liquids worked well as invisible inks?

2. Which liquids didn't?

3. Did some inks become visible faster than others when exposed to heat?

4. Let's say that your safety depended on using the best invisible ink. Which one would you choose?

14

1 Squeeze the juice from a lemon half into a small glass.

2 Dip a cotton swab into the juice. Use it to write a short message on a piece of paper.

3 Let the message dry.

4 Now hold the paper close to, but not touching, the shining lightbulb.

5 See what happens.

6 Repeat the process using milk as your invisible ink.

TIP
A lightbulb might not be hot enough to reveal your invisible ink. You can also iron the paper using the lowest setting. Be sure to get help from an adult. And turn off the steam function!

The Science behind the Fun

Why does it work? Good question! Both lemon juice and milk contain acid. When the liquids dry, the acid remains on the paper. When held near the heat of the light bulb, the acid turns brown, revealing the secret message.

☆ EVEN COOLER!
Write messages with vinegar, water, onion juice, **diluted** honey, and other fruit juices. Note which ones work as invisible inks and which ones don't.

Science at Work

People have used invisible inks for secret communications since ancient times. Inks can be made from simple kitchen ingredients or high-tech compounds. Some invisible inks are revealed by heat. Some inks change color when an acid or a **base** is added, causing a chemical reaction. Other inks are visible only when viewed under **ultraviolet** light.

Periscope Fun

TIME: ABOUT 90 MINUTES

MATERIALS

2 half-gallon (1.9 l) milk or juice cartons

scissors or utility knife

tape

hot-glue gun

2 pieces of cardboard about 7 × 3 inches (18 × 8 cm)

2 small mirrors about 3 × 3 inches (8 × 8 cm)

A periscope uses mirrors to help you see things that are out of your line of sight. In this activity, you'll make periscopes to see around a corner and underwater. Now that's some tricky business!

PHYSICS

THINK LIKE A SCIENTIST!

1. In your science journal, write how your periscopes work.

2. Make simple diagrams that explain your designs. Look at the diagram on page 18 if you need help.

3. Draw maps of where you used your periscopes. Note what you could and couldn't see using the devices.

17

1 Cut off the top and bottom ends of the cartons. Tape the two cartons end-to-end to make a long, tube-like box.

2 At one end of the box, cut a three-inch-square (8 cm) opening. Cut another opening at the other end, but on the opposite side. It should be the same size as the first opening.

3 Fold and tape the two pieces of cardboard into right triangles.

4 Glue a mirror to the long, slanted side of each triangle.

The Science behind the Fun

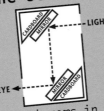

A periscope works because light bounces off a mirror in a straight line. The mirrors in your periscope work together. They bounce the image to your eye in a Z pattern.

Science at Work

One of the best-known uses of periscopes is in submarines. A sub crew uses a periscope to see what's happening at the surface when they are underwater. They pull the device back into the body of the sub when it's not in use. Submarine periscopes are complex, using prisms instead of mirrors. Some modern submarines use newer technologies instead of periscopes.

5 When the glue is dry, place the triangles in the box corners. They should be opposite the openings. The short side of the triangles should be against the ends and sides of the box. The mirrors should be facing outward.

6 Take your periscope outside to see how it works. Hide behind a corner. Hold the device so that one of its openings sticks out past the corner. Align that opening with the object you wish to view. Look into the other opening. If needed, adjust the mirrors inside the periscope so you can see the object.

EVEN COOLER!

You can even use a periscope to see underwater. Here's how.

MATERIALS

half-gallon (1.9 l) plastic milk jug   heavy-duty rubber band   scissors

bubble bath or dish soap   large tub of water   plastic wrap

1. Cut the top and the bottom off the milk jug. Leave the handle intact.

2. Stretch a large piece of plastic wrap over the bottom opening. Make sure the plastic is pulled tightly in place. Secure the plastic with the rubber band.

3. Fill the tub with water and add the bubble bath. Stir it up so you can't see the bottom of the tub. Close your eyes and drop a few coins into the tub.

4. Hold the periscope by the handle. Push the plastic-covered end beneath the bubbles. Don't push the entire device underwater.

5. Look through the periscope to see through the bubbles and find your coins. The water will magnify everything you look at. So, the coins may appear slightly larger than they are!

Mirror Gear

TIME: ABOUT 1 HOUR

MATERIALS

REARVIEW MIRRORS
tape

sunglasses

2 small mirrors, each about 1 inch (2.5 cm) in diameter or smaller

EXTREME CHANNEL SURFING
television with a remote control

mirror

friend

MIRROR MESSAGES
marker

paper

mirror

Mirrors have long been handy tools in the spy trade. In these activities, you will use common mirrors in some rather uncommon ways!

PHYSICS

THINK LIKE A SCIENTIST!
In **espionage** circles, the clever **gizmos** that field agents use are called sneakies. Think about the different ways you used mirrors in these activities. Then brainstorm with a friend to invent ways you could use mirrors in undercover work. Write down your ideas in your science journal. Make sketches to illustrate your designs.

20

Rearview Mirrors

Turn your sunglasses into some super-clever spyware.

1 Make two small loops of tape with the sticky side facing out.

2 Place the tape loops inside the sunglasses. Put them on the frame near the stems if there is room. Otherwise, put them on the lenses.

3 Stick a small mirror to each tape loop.

4 Put on the glasses and start walking. Look in the left mirror, then the right mirror. What do you see?

Science at Work

Usually, if you can see a person in a mirror, that person can also see you. But one-way mirrors are different. They reflect some light and let some light pass through.

Sometimes one-way mirrors are placed between a darkly lit room and a brightly lit room. The people in the brightly lit space see themselves in the mirror. The people in the darkly lit space see through to the other side. Sometimes police use one-way mirrors to observe criminals. Security staff in stores may use them to observe customers.

Extreme Channel Surfing

Use a mirror to change the television channel from another room!

1 Look at the front of the television to locate the small light detector. It may be round or square. This is the spot where the television receives signals from the remote control. It's also your target.

2 Stand outside the television room with the remote control.

3 Have your friend hold the mirror. You should be able to see the television in the mirror.

4 Now aim the remote control at the target in the mirror. Press the channel up or down button. What happens?

The Science behind the Fun

The remote control shoots invisible light to the light detector on the television. This invisible light is called **infrared** light. It moves in straight lines and bounces off the mirror just like other light. That's what lets you change the channel from afar.

Mirror Messages

Here's a simple way to make a secret message.

1 Write a message on a piece of paper with the marker.

2 Now flip over the paper and trace the letters from the other side. This is your secret message.

3 To read the message, hold it in front of a mirror. What do you see?

4 Now look at the original message in the mirror. What do you see?

Science at Work

A mirror is a smooth surface that reflects light and images of objects. The reflective properties of mirrors make them useful tools in general science. For example, large, bowl-shaped mirrors in reflective telescopes focus light from faraway objects. Mirrors also help increase the power of light in **lasers**. The humble mirror has gone high tech!

Match Game

TIME: ABOUT 30 MINUTES

MATERIALS
pencil
transparent tape
paper
magnifying glass
family members
or friends

No two people's fingerprints are the same. In this activity, you'll compare prints from several people to find a match. Is that a loop, an arch, or a **whorl**? You'll soon find out!

BIOLOGY

Bridge

Alexei

Pam

ean

Chris

Liz

Tracy

Anders

THINK LIKE A SCIENTIST!

It's time to gather some data. Find a few people to take fingerprints from. They can be family members, classmates, or friends. Record their names and the kind of print each person has.

Here's a sample table to get you started. Make a similar table in your science journal. What does the data you gathered tell you? Which kind of print was the most common? Which kind appeared least often?

Name	Kind of print
Anders	whorl
Chris	loop
Pam	loop
Tracy	arc

24

1 Scribble on a piece of paper with a pencil. Create a black mark at least 1 inch square (2.5 cm).

2 Rub your index finger in the pencil mark.

3 Put a piece of tape over your finger and press down.

4 Pull the tape off and put it on a piece of paper. You should be able to see your fingerprint.

5 Study the print. Compare it with the examples on the next page to see what kind of print you have.

The Science behind the Fun

Take a close look at your fingertips. You'll see the skin has raised ridges on it. These ridges can trap natural oils or other matter. Then, when you touch a surface, the combination of the ridges and the matter creates a fingerprint. Because everyone's ridges are unique, fingerprints can be used to identify people. Over the years, scientists have developed systems for classifying fingerprints. Loops, arches, and whorls are from the Henry system, for example. Today we use computers to analyze prints.

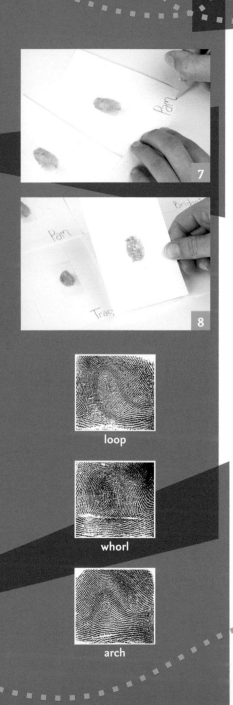

loop

whorl

arch

6 Now take two prints each from several friends' right index fingers.

7 Mark each person's name on one of the prints. Leave the second print nameless.

8 Mix up the unmarked prints and choose one. Try to match it to one of the named prints.

9 Continue matching sets for even more practice!

Science at Work

Forensic scientists look for fingerprints at crime scenes. They dust fine aluminum powder over surfaces where fingerprints are likely to be. When they find a print, they can "lift" it with tape. Then they take the print back to the lab for study. Photographs are also commonly used to record prints.

Countries all over the world use fingerprints to identify people. However, countries use different systems to classify prints. A certain number of points must be identical to consider two prints a match. Countries also have different standards for how many points must be identical.

It's Alarming!

TIME: ABOUT 30 MINUTES

Security alarms come in all shapes and sizes. This chair alarm is fashioned from a basic circuit with a small buzzer. The alarm buzzes when someone sits down in the chair. Now you'll know when someone sits at your desk. Busted!

PHYSICS

THINK LIKE A SCIENTIST!
How can you redesign the alarm to use it in another location, such as a doorway? Sketch your design on a piece of paper. Then try building it. How does it work? Tinker with other designs for different situations.

1 Fold a piece of paper down the middle.

2 Unfold the paper and build the circuit shown here on the paper. You will need to cut one alligator wire in half. Tape each element of the circuit in place.

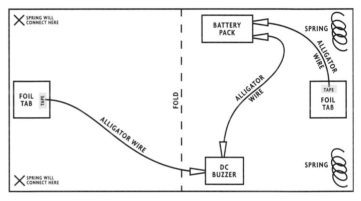

3 Position the two foil tabs so they touch when the paper is folded. This is the key to your alarm system.

4 Make simple springs by winding two pipe cleaners around a pencil. Leave a straight section at each end of each spring. Take the springs off of the pencils. Tape the ends of the pipe cleaner springs to the paper as shown.

5 Place the alarm on a chair seat, covering it with a pillow.

6 Test your alarm system to see if it works.

7 Adjust the parts of the alarm as needed.

8

8 Reset the alarm with the pillow on top. Go wait within hearing distance of the alarm.

9 See what happens when someone sits on the chair!

The Science behind the Fun

An electric current is a flow of electrons through wires and electronic components. A circuit is a closed path that an electric current flows through. In this case, the buzzer uses electricity from the battery. The circuit is completed when the foil tabs touch. This occurs when the person sits on the alarm and compresses the springs.

Science at Work

Security alarms can be hardwired or wireless. A home security alarm is triggered when someone opens a door or window. This breaks the circuit and triggers the alarm. Other alarms use **infrared** light to detect motion. The alarm goes off if someone breaks the beam of light.

Conclusion

These top secret activities were designed to do one at a time. But once you know how they all work, you can combine them for some super spy-science fun! First make a spy kit from an old suitcase or a cardboard box. Put all your spy gear together so everything is handy. Don't label the kit, since you want to be undercover!

Then work with a friend to plan a series of spy challenges for some friends to solve. You could call it a spy scavenger hunt or an obstacle course. For example, start with a message written in invisible ink. This message will tell them what their next spy challenge is.

Solving these spy-science challenges requires creative thinking based on what you know about how the world works. It also involves answering some interesting questions. Sounds like fun!

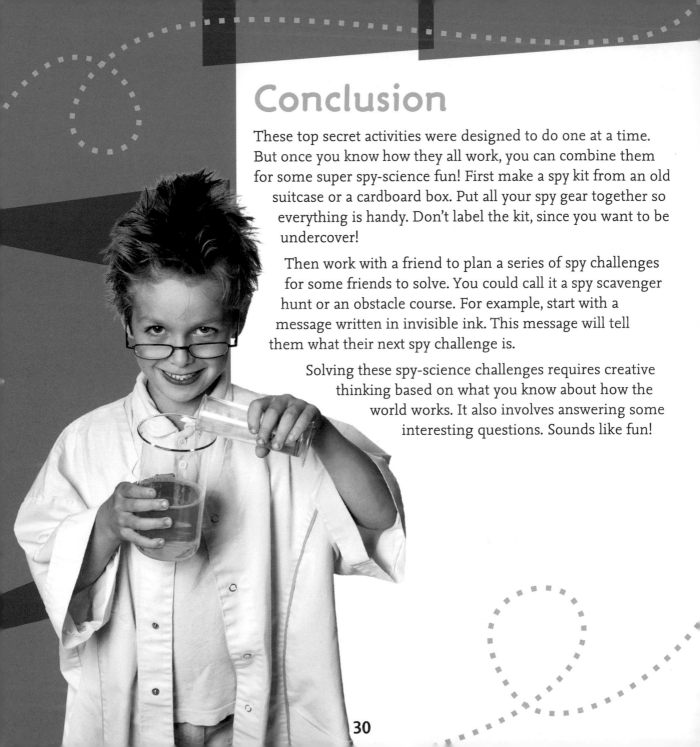

Glossary

base – a chemical substance that neutralizes acids, tastes bitter, and becomes slippery when mixed with water.

cipher – secret writing in which the letters are scrambled according to a key.

DC – abbreviation for direct current, an electric current that flows in one direction only. Batteries provide direct current.

dilute – to make thinner or weaker by adding a liquid such as water.

espionage – the practice of spying.

essential – very important or necessary.

forensic science – science that helps answer legal questions.

gizmo – a gadget.

incandescent – an electric light bulb that produces light when a fine wire is heated by electrical current.

infrared – electromagnetic radiation with a longer wavelength than visible light but a shorter wavelength than microwaves.

laser – a device that makes an intense, thin beam of light.

sleuth – a detective.

ultraviolet – a type of light that cannot be seen with the human eye. It has a shorter wavelength than visible light but a longer wavelength than X-rays.

whorl – a curl or swirl. In a whorl fingerprint, the central lines make at least one complete circle.

WEB SITES

To learn more about the science of spying, visit ABDO Publishing Company on the World Wide Web at **www.abdopublishing.com.** Web sites about spy science are featured on our Book Links page. These links are routinely monitored and updated to provide the most current information available.

Index